'The two of us is all there is,
The rest is just a dream.'

RS

I

It doesn't make the world go 'round
But it seems like I've found
A way out.

Peacefully on my own, alone
Hidden away from the drone
All around.

Dreadful faces and voices
Choke the life from my choices
To go on.

Shudder myself to sleep
It's the only way to keep
Me alive.

II

Designing 4
Aim seems to change from the beginning to
the end.

Implementing 5
Very professional attitude

Interpreting 4
No detailed reason for choice of stats.

Communication 3
I don't know what to say.

Total 16

Fail.

III

Go into the bathroom. Roses are free.
To those who beg for the chain 'round their
neck.
Mrs Rocastle did it once and swore
That she loved it. She would.
Yuri Geller spoon trick suspension toilet
Execution.

She still can't speak. She's an idiot.
30 years of wasted life. She has to eat
With spoons now, her forks are stuck
In the chain. There's no room for her neck.
Ecstasy of scowling down
Seeing feet dangle off ground.
If the spoons will hold.

What a pain in the neck. Act it out, close the
door.
Don't want neighbours to hear a scream.
Can't afford perpetual shellshock.
The roses are free.

IV

Being right by a beach
I saw a wave so huge
It filled the red sky.
I stood in a garage and watched it
Flood over streets. Cry.

With a girl, I saw another;
Bigger, darker, deeper.
With nowhere to hide, we dived
Under a car. Nowhere to go.
Nowhere to die.

I remember being by the cliff.
High and dry.

V

Dawn. Beginning. A nothing.
You mean nothing. Beginning.
Sharp birds in an endless spiral of air.
At least for a short while. Now, nothing.

Tools are blunt, yet kind.
But there. They're here. A beginning.
In the distance, the guitar is touched
Only faint. Trouble looms then fades.

Dread then pleasure. At least for a short
while.

No-one hears, but later they do.
Birds form. Obvious. Swirling. Fight fight.
Let them all, especially one, hear the
unstoppable
Sound of a guitar. Mine.

Tools sharper, somehow sharper. Birds
disperse.

VI

I'm watching TV
And still she watches me.
I look through the screen
Into a rare dream.
A world where nothing matters.
You know.
Nothing really matters.

Imagine, you could be there.

When I'm like this
It bugs. Really bugs here.
She's floating now.
She can do that.
When she's bugged, she floats.
I can too, but I'm not bugged.
I'm in a place
Where nothing matters.

I'm here with you now
Not like her.

'You floating doesn't bother me...'
See, she doesn't listen.
She's bugged.

Nothing wrong with circles.
Knew that at school.
Thought it was stability.
Endless perimeter. One sided.

One sided security's changed.
Knew that at school.
Life's now one big circle.
You and I trapped within.

Circle threatens to crack.
Opportunities, different paths.
Settle into rhythm.
Circle closes, shuts off.

A way out of perpetual mire.
A second side, a third.
Shattered once and for all.
A way. Circle-jerk. Jerk off.

VII

Dreams of the end haunt me,
This time it's the death cloud
Enveloping everyone.

I peer through empty gates
Of a blue stadium
Nobody knows their fate is here.

I run to wooded hills
Look over my shoulder.
The cloud. The end has begun.

A small boy flies a helicopter
A rescue. An escape.
He crashes hopelessly and dies.

The cloud roles forward.
Like a burning cigar.
The end, never remembered.

VIII

Desperation hangs over me
As the gallows creek.
Fate smiles a mile
Of a well-beaten road
To nowhere.
The future turns and walks away.

I was their first customer;
Plaques of Diana adorn walls,
Eastern in tatty seaside halls.

I'm with a black haired girl
She knows me. I don't.
As we sit, I feel new. Pure.
I remember nothing else. Sure.

It was this morning.

IX

A Green fly walks to me
It thinks, 'I need to see
What makes you,' the tick
Said 'tick' as it flew
Away.

X

This one's ours.
This one's hours.

Yours sincerely
Roly Poly
Big one really
Slowly holy
Sincerely roly
Really holy
Big yours.

Huge jaws.

XI

I milked a heart shake
And made the call to you.
I knew I really didn't want to.

A tremble in your voice
Gave it all away.
A chat to save for another day.

You waited to hear what
You already knew.
I told you I loved you.

Another chance gone begging
A banquet for a cure.
Placebo for the unsure.

XII

If the sky were to fall in
And the moon to fall down
And my tears were like the rain
Of a foolish old clown
It wouldn't matter.

If these clouds all explode
And the sun, deathly grey
Pours more grim pain
Over a pointless, tearful day
It wouldn't matter.

If the sudden winds of change
And the pulling air of fears
Were to stop my frantic breath
And dry up my endless tears
It wouldn't matter.

If the whole world were to say
You're not needed any more
I'd let myself fall away
Through the inviting death door
It really wouldn't matter.

XIII

It's like
It's like a tunnel.
Darkness is everywhere, but it's good
And imperative.

The glorious light at the end
The Reward, the ultimate is near
And yet so far.

If you hold my hand, I'll hold yours.
The tunnel is dark and desperate
But we see the light and
Somehow, inexplicably, brighter.
Sharper. Bigger.

Without faith the darkness swallows whole
And that light shatters
Like an exploding bulb.

If we slip,
If we slip, I'll hold your hand. And you'll
hold mine.
The end is not near, but it's not far away.
You know by now. The rest's up to you.

XIV

Just look at me,
Don't touch. Trembling.
A spinning spiral of expectation
Taunts us all, sucks us.

If we touch, we touch a whirlpool
Of words meaning fear, out of control
Down a clown's helter skelter.
Just look at me.

A desire for more adds to the split
Which greets us all
With wild, spinning palms.
When we don't touch, we are closest.
Anticipate. Think. Step for more
And fall.

XV

Get in on the taker, always been a faker
Of tans.
LA Laker, a three point taker
With plans.
A cooler shaker, please forsake her.
Again.

XVI

Like an ancient stone woman
Whose creaking neck
Steers her to eternal oblivion.
To turn, to face her life mirror.

A moth smacks the window
For the tenth time.
And reality floats through hard glass,
Showing us a shallow way.

When a moth gives up,
We understand that reality can never be
Reached.

XVII

My love you are here now
And each passing hour chimes
The loss of time, so empty.
This room could be full
With a thousand stars,
Each one a shining reminder
That there can only ever be one you.
You are here now my love
It's strange that I feel warmed.
The freedom I feel is here to remind me
Of the times we spend alone. Apart.
If fate decides that now is a mere pause
In the dark, give me you guiding hand
Only you can fill the void
That grabs and pulls at me,
Persuading me that nowhere
Is better than here.
One day, all around me can be us;
Feel us,
Smell us,
Be us,
As one.

XVIII

Of course the impossible happens.
If you want it to.
Inhibitions. Fears. Doubts. All stand.
Obstructions, so madness can change that.
The path is cleared, laden with gold,
And time stands still.

XIX

Walking asleep in the rain
I see you in pain

Full of fear and sadness
Of what never became.

Pity, wary, shame.

XX

Night - the lights pass me
By. I float on sand but feel

People crying at me as I start
Burning bridges under water.

The glass falls in a black bag
I watch and hear my past shatter.

Lost faces weep at how long,
Brighter and younger things were.

Dress me up and sob all day
At what I seem and am not.

A glass envelope sends a letter;
Clear, cut and shiny. Smashed.

To pieces.

XXI

You gave me flowers for hours.
Sweet flowers, bunched blooms.
Floral gifts, endless shifts.

You wouldn't stop, you gave me more.
I bagged them up, I smiled.
In my pockets, on the floor.

I swept more up and kissed you
On the face.

XXII

You get up me like pollen
On a cold winter's day.

You get on me like a carousel
Out of season, shut down.

You get under me like the weather
When I'm in a sick bed.

You get over me quite quickly.
Actually.

XXIII

You're just the perfect girl.

You are.

XXIV

A long time ago
When I was a pear
I always dreamed
I'd fall in love
And not from a tree.

A short time ago
When I was a plum
I knew that love
Was soon to come
All over me.

At this moment
I am you, you are me
And I'm glad I'm not
A plum or pear –
You'd be here,
And I'd be there.

XXV

She read my script
Saliva dripping off her chin.
'I must have the lead role,
I can be your star!'
My life script is a mere mirror
Observed. A reflection for her self
Pity.
She was stunning up there in lights;
Pulling strings, screams, whispers.
A costume closing me down.

I still view her script
For me, the improvised, a cameo.
Amateur, peripheral, a short term effect.
Now, she stinks of jealous lies
Like scripture in a strange tongue.
I would never learn.
She struts on stage, well-rehearsed
And fakes the applause of a critic.
I close as I clap too.

XXVI

I love you, I love you, I do.
Tell me something new.
I love you too, I really do.
I don't know how or why,
But I'll love you 'til I die.

It will be now, it will be soon.
It will be later, forever more.
The death tune of the moon,
Rocks us on, smitten to the core.

XXVII

You, always needed it.
You, always dictated time.
You, absolutely desperate.
You, sublime.

It always needed you.
Time always dictated you.
Absolutely desperate you.
Sublime you.

XXVIII

Skin deep is shallow as skin.
Push a syringe into your great big head.
Know how it feels. Cry baby.

Skip through a flake field with wild dogs
Trip on a cartridge. Fuck rock.
Christ, did you see that?

Syringe Head's playground again.
He'll never learn that needles in a head
stack
Can be real pain in the ass.

Cry baby. Tell 'em to shoot him, up. At last.
Syringe Head's dead.

XXIX

That hole speaks volumes
Like the mauve, it blossoms
Surrounded with a chain.
Prepared, clean.
Cut the brown
So grow with it.

XXX

My heart is a playground.
They run and shout
And pound my floors.
A bell will always send them home.

XXXI

As the laboured breath of a train
Is lifted away
On the soothing breeze,
Hair envelopes my pale face,
Covering a happy, lying smile.

Like a mask.

As the life of the town
Breathes onwards
Below my thoughtless gaze,
My mind turns once more
To my love, your lips, our smile.

Under a tree.

As the eager travellers
Walk upwards, ants
Towards the highest peak,
My hopes return to warm me
Like the sun, trapped

In the desperate sky.

XXXII

The things that you and I see
As milestones
Come and go
Like hazy road signs
In a private thunderstorm.

Just keep driving.

XXXIII

I look up at the sparse clouds and reflect on
how quickly they change shape and move
on to new skies. I look around at vibrant
red smells that fill my mind and overwhelm
my soul. Soon it will be gone, fallen from
glory, awaiting the Dawn of a new Spring.

The touch of rich earth crumbles through
my aging fingers and falls in patterns new
to surround yet more life; a bronzed, pollen
filled creation, an ocean enveloping islands
of beauty. I look up to see the sun,
darkened by a mass of cloud. Amber and
ready.

A tired cat walks by, baffled by mankind
scribbling the obvious onto a form that
dwelled here once.

Before destruction moved in, noisily.

XXXIV

Too late. Just too late.
'Be unfaithful,' she pleads.
'I need a reason to go
I need a reason to show
That you're not everything.'

'Be unfaithful,' she screams.
'Otherwise, the reason has gone,
Forced to stay forever
And a day.
That might be more than I can take.'

She's starting to sway.
I won't go away.
'Be unfaithful. Be unfaithful,' she chants.
And the tears are falling. Not pain.
Relief. She knows I won't.

She knows who I am. It's just too late.
To turn back.

XXXV

The huge man stands on the chests
Of two naked lovers, impaled on bone.
His four arms hold swords and scissors
Laced with dull gleaming black pearls.
A severed head sleeps, tugged by hair
That no longer grows there.
The man offers a white swollen flower
As he stoops, allowing serpents
To drop from his head, probing flesh.
The bones crunch as a thousand faces
Smile and snigger at the scene below.
Faces suspended in air, connected.

I don't know what this man sees,
But he feels the warmth of his hair
Coiling and eating
The two dead lovers there.

XXXVI

A woman with long blonde hair
Dressed in red, had appeared to him.
She gave an ultimatum.

'I'm sure I don't understand what these
options entail.'
She asked how he wanted to spend the
time
Between lives.

The woman repeated her choices.

Harmony or wandering.

XXXVII

Sitting in the waiting room
Weight and self-pity.
Quick back to a womb.

(Tranquility.)

You think it's a game
Consequences.
Peace and inability.

(Dumb.)

Last night, or when.
Unable to stop birth
No need to be.

(Here.)

XXXVIII

A fly struggles with a web
A spider smiles too
We all cry.

A fly on a windscreen
Curses its luck
We all sigh.

A fly in a trap
Venus just shrugs
We know why.

A pretty fly
For a shite guy.
We all die.

XXXIX

What do you do
When the sky falls in?
Ask for mom? Cling to dad?
I know how it's gonna be.

A lot of people won't. Sleeping. Dying.
Digging.
They'll just go. To a place in the sky
Where the sky once was.
The sky's down here and we're up there.
Floating.

Looking down at the sky.
What would you do?
No ground to step on.
No grass to play on.
No road to crash on.

Endless souls swaying. Longing.
Reversal, how things were.
We're all dead. And now I'm scared.

XXXX

The winds of change are much stronger
today
They push aside the clouds that stayed
Around yesterday.
And make way for a chapter of the new
That troubled the minds of others too.
As they pass over their skies.

Whose cloud will you be?
When I'm gone?
A cover for a place
Where his sun once shone.

It's been so calm recently
Today must mean something...

XXXXI

Without you
The countdown has begun,
And so have the dreams.
Dreams that fill me
With dread, fear, terror...
Dreams of betrayal, stupidity.
More fear.

Consciously, I know better,
Unconsciously, I know nothing.
Subconsciously, I know the worst.

The fear of pain, the fear of distance
Over love, eternal love.
The dreams are hazy,
Vague narcotic memory of betrayal
And apathy.
You didn't care.

XXXXII

I've got a Wurlitzer special tattoo
On my ass.
Video priest screaming out
High mass.
Sick school girls rolling around
On the floor
Jehovah's witness knocking
At my door.
Redneck sucking life
From a can.
Naked women making me
A man.
Big brown bush.
Schizophrenic.

XXXXIII

The air, cool breeze that washes
Over me, cleans my ebbing mind.
The anxious children rest in rows
Their pens meandering, unsigned.

The future sits heavily on their backs
Judging work with a critical nod.
I remember their fear too well
Our naïve mutterings to an invisible god.

If only I could cry and plead
With them, make them understand
Destiny is a cruel, grinning man
That plays the winning hand.

The breeze, cool air that washes
Over me, cleans my ebbing mind.
The relieved children leave in rows
Redundant pens and their fates resigned.

XXXXIV

Two snakes, coiled to conceive
Serpentine energy, you received.
What do you think, wooden girl?
A rigid face, two circles, a pearl
To freeze you there forever
In your state of stringent bliss.

Will the serpent ever grow?
Will that face ever show
The noises you will make,
The pleasure you may take
Being as this, long, long ago
In stern, uncompromising joy.

XXXXV

Expressions of passion
Inconceivable energy
Never in one fashion
Immense given bodies.

Symbolic cremation
Limitless libido
Aureoles of flame
Demonstrative copulation.

Reservoired progenies enhance
Allegories. Absorbed.
Our shamans dance
With projected fantasy.

XXXXVI

The female wisdom with bowls of food

Impaled on a destroyer, whipping lewd.

Standing on a body of pearls, gold and hard

Lifted away by dragons – twisted, jarred.

XXXXVII

Two naked lovers sit on grass.
Five huge trees protect them both.
Seven probing tubes, each other pass.
They use them, smiling under oath.

Above them, on a vast broad branch,
An old recumbent man is talking
To a tired, crying lioness.
An initiation begins.

XXXXVIII

Without sight, my mind wonders
And I see everything
Big, full and swollen.

With sight, my brain is focused.
You see nothing, small and shrunk,
Skimming me nowhere.

A benefit.

XXXXIX

We crossed town, falling
Into a huge boat, full of colours.
Balloons, balls, floating
On menacing dark waters.

I saved you once.
You saved me twice.

Talking behind curtains
As mists descend outside.
We now lie prone and hide.
You are the one.

L

Stark banality,
Inadequacy
Falseness
Of every day.
Images
From a cage,
Surrounding
Our sublime
Indulgence.

A reflection
Of the permanent
A hologram
Of reality –
An icon
Your own image
My dancing girl,
Divine.

LI

How often will I dream
Of this field by the stream?
Where we lay down our home
And let eager minds roam.

How often will I smile
As we walked for a mile
To find somewhere to hide
To listen and confide?

The answer it seems
For our stream and these dreams –
Go with your heart's needs.
Sow and reap your own seeds...

LII

Sharing symbolic sanctity
Avoiding quick scurry to finish,

You become a paradigm
Of conceived, divine ecstasy.

Feeling appetite and relief,
A cheap external explanation,

Orgasm becomes punctuation
For a longer, stranger story.

Attraction is not appetite,
Feeling is not a reaction,

But a carefully nurtured creation
Protracted joy embraced,
Demanding self-abnegation.

My libido and idle imaginings
Fixed on one eternal, changeless light.
Swallowed like a cup of warm water
Through the surface of a burning lake.

LIII

Claustrophobia.
People, fumes (of)
Consumed alcohol.
Transport.
Going home (we)
Together. Alone.

Exultation.
I need (you)
With me.
You can't doubt (me)
Or ever fear
Betrayal.

Perfect moments
(like) this
should confirm (us)
We become us.

LIV

Where I went today, the sky was blue
And everything was perfect.
Now I sit here and I see one,
Big awesome star rising above
A black line.

I'm cold but I fear nothing,
My nudity only adds to the power
I feel as I gaze over the scape
Before me.

I hear the stream that obsessed me
Only hours ago and I ponder –
The infinity of this moment
And then you.

Away from me, I turn to see
My lover drifting over things
From long ago. She is warm, content,
Bed of blossom.

You are my serene Ophelia,
Your curling hair spread over you
Soft floral pillow, waiting for sleep,
Dreams of now.

As I stop, I join her, with that star
Watching over us both. I can't wait.
So why is it that every day
Can't be today?

LV

A heaven that awaits heroes
Full of celestial imagery.
Symbolically married
To this rehearsal of life.

Erotic function.

LVI

Manifestations
Of
Sexuality.
Appetite
And
Relief – banal.

Cheap external explanations of sex,
impoverished rationalisation of the infinite
complex. My hedonistic focus on erotic
possession gives physical radiance.

Form
Is
Emptiness.
Emptiness
Is
Form.

LVII

Temporary isolation, enforced separation
Hammers a steel wedge between us.
I float onwards, away to
Appalling lands of misery.

I only remember what you were;
Distant already, vanishing
Over my sinking shoulders.

I almost resent you for letting me go.
I lie – grounded, wingless, spineless.

I thought you'd ring tonight.

You always do.

LVIII

Here it is again,
Another piece of a dream
Unearthed.
I told myself
I didn't have to be so afraid.
I stood naked for a moment
On a purple path,
Ran forward
And leapt into the water.
Even as I flew,
It occurred to me
That the last time
I jumped in like this,
The air tasted of thick honey too.
As I cut the surface,
I felt that my hapless heart
Had fallen out of my open mouth
And sunk to the green depths,
Hiding from the icy water
Underneath its bed.
My chest tightened
As I drifted deeper,
Cold intensity clamping itself
To my body,
Stabbing and pinching at my chest,
Arms and back.

The ruby weeds and thick slime
Stopped my aimless fall
And I pushed off them,
Arrowing upward,
A blade cutting through the water
That had threatened to crush me.
As I broke the surface,
I felt my blue heart surge past
And reclaim the place it owned,
Pulling on the warm air
That wrapped around me.
I tasted the water,
Pure and sharp,
Allowing it to consume
And eat me
From within.
I asked my heart to help me,
And it did,
Still aware that my body was floating
In the prickly cold.
My nudity urged me to relax,
Not an exposure,
But an offering –
To stay there.
The sun came to me,
Through trees of gold
And persuaded me to drift over
To the crystalline raft that bobbed

Effortlessly in the sun's hue.
I lay on my back
And allowed ripples
Of need
To carry me
To you.

LIX

'Memories are feelings that affect us from within. They move with us.'

 Always.

23291700R00033

Printed in Poland
by Amazon Fulfillment
Poland Sp. z o.o., Wrocław